CONFRONTATI

PHOTOGRAPHS OF THE PHILIPPINES AND THE UNITED STATES

CROSSINGS AND

1 8 9 8 - 1 9 9 8

CONVERGENCE

Enrique B. de la Cruz and Pearlie Rose S. Baluyut
Editors and Curators
With
Rico J. Reyes, *Co-Curator*

A Co-Publication of
The UCLA Asian American Studies Center and The UCLA Southeast Asia Program
1998

Published by the
UCLA Asian American Studies Center and the UCLA Southeast Asia Program
Los Angeles, California

Publisher's Cataloging-in-Publication Data
Main entry under title:

Enrique B. de la Cruz, Pearlie Rose S. Baluyut

Confrontations, Crossings, and Convergence: Photographs of the Philippines and the United States, 1898-1998

p. cm.

ISBN 0-9340522-7-1 (paper)

1. Filipino Americans—California—Los Angeles. 2. Photography—History. 3. Photography—Philippine-U.S.—Exhibitions. 4. Filipinos—Philippines. 5. Filipino Americans—California—History. 6. World War, 1939-1945—United States.

I. Title. II. de la Cruz, Enrique B.; Baluyut, Pearlie Rose S.; Rico J. Reyes III. UCLA Asian American Studies Center; UCLA Southeast Asia Program.

Date of first publication: October 1998

Library of Congress Catalog Card Number: 98-75033

Printed by Edwards Brothers, Inc., Ann Arbor, Michigan, in the United States of America

10 9 8 7 6 5 4 3 2 1

Book Design/Production: Abraham Ferrer

TABLE OF CONTENTS

A "trick photo" showing the same man in five different exposures

Philippines, ca. 1930s
Anonymous
Jonathan Best Private Collection

THE POWER OF PICTURES

Photographs are never 'evidence' of history; they are themselves the historical.

—John Tagg, *The Burden of Representation*

T he signing of the Treaty of Paris in 1898 significantly altered the historic direction of the Philippines. As it sealed four centuries of Spanish colonialism, it also signaled the emergence of American empire on Philippine soil. Colonial efforts to render 'familiar' the distant archipelago and its people enlisted many scholars in the field of anthropology, history, medicine, and linguistics. One hundred years later, attempts to understand the complex relationship of the Philippines and the United States have led to the reconfiguration of the empirical frame. To this theoretical construct of domination and resistance, the element of negotiation is introduced; to the process of textual narration, we add the experience of visual encounters. The aim of the exhibition and the companion book, hence, is to articulate the complexity of Philippine-U.S. history through photography.

■

During the Renaissance, virtual image production came in the form of a darkened chamber with a small opening in one wall that received light from the outside and projected an inverted image of an object on the opposite wall. This ancestral optical device known as the *camera obscura* was considered an instrument of evidence—an embodiment of truth. By the nineteenth century, pioneers such as Niépce, Daguerre, Herschel, Talbot, Nadar, and Eastman further developed the apparatus and/or discovered methods of chemically preserving the image, thereby opening a new frontier in visual representation.

Although research in the history of photography in the Philippines is still in its infancy, vintage stereoscopic pictures of the Tinguian tribeswomen of Abra taken by an anonymous French engineer visiting the South Seas in the 1860s reveal photography's far-reaching legacy. Besides the French explorers, physicians, traders, and scholars, photography was popularized in the Philippines by the burgeoning middle class. Whereas before the development of dry and wet plates the members of the elite society contented themselves with painted miniature portraits and *letras y figuras* as forms of social advertisements, photographs slowly eclipsed these traditional folk representations as evidenced by the mushrooming of studios in Manila.

Despite early Orientalist attempts to exoticize the Philippines, it was not until the arrival of the Americans that the former was reproduced in an unprecedented scale. Portraits of Filipino aristocrats, street vendors, and mountain tribes, scenes of rural and urban life, and images of ceremonial gatherings and tropical landscape appeared as book illustrations or as picture postcards which American soldiers, missionaries, and teachers in the Philippines shared with their families and friends in the United States. Indeed, photography sustained not only the pursuit of scientific knowledge, but triggered an age of modern mass tourism and cultural commodification.

Under American colonial rule, the photographs of the Philippines and its people were regarded as ocular templates of truth—scientific records of both the ideal and the stereotype. Yet these so-called 'black-and-white' evidence were always colored by the personal intentions or political ideology of the photographer/institution. Although often subjected to racial ridicule, it was not entirely a matter of surrender on the photographed subject's behalf. Over the years, picture-taking itself became an occasion of intervention; at other times, it was a calculated embrace, a desirable collaboration, and an urgent negotiation.

This introductory essay serves only as a point of departure. Rather than textually recapitulate the last century of Philippine-U.S. relations, the images in the exhibition and book are the ones tasked with the burden of representation and narration. Loquacious and never silent, photographs are versed narrators that tell many stories and, simultaneously, pose historical riddles. As such, they no longer remain as objective, unchanging evidence of history, but are encounters in the making.

To engage the reader/viewer in a fuller discourse, we have added forty-nine more photographs to the fifty images that were exhibited. The book, however, preserves the original thematic organization of the exhibition: "Spectacle and Surveillance" explores the United States' uncanny display and disciplining of Filipino bodies at the turn of the century; "Diaspora, Struggles, and Survival" surveys the experiences of Filipinos in the United States and the Americans in the Philippines; "Resistance and Collaboration" critically examines the shifts in Filipino American relations during the Spanish-American War, the Philippine-American War, and the Second World War; and, finally, "Closures, Fractures, and Parallels" revisits the U.S.-supported Marcos and post-Marcos era and reflects on the path that Philippine-U.S. history has taken.

Although the four themes follow a certain chronology insofar as their sequence is concerned, temporal crossovers, fractures, and parallels occur under each theme. In fact, the element of time is used not to create order, but to encourage overlaps, ultimately blurring the thematic boundaries and disrupting the temporal continuum. Rather than explain, the photographs seek to problematize the relationship of the Philippines and the United States while engaging the viewer in a dialogue that further reevaluates this complexity. In this power-game of looking, being looked at, and, most importantly, looking back, photographs signify the dynamic shifts—domination, resistance, and negotiation—in relations. And here lies the power of pictures.

Pearlie Rose S. Baluyut
September 1998

ACKNOWLEDGMENTS

Undertaking a Philippine centennial photograph exhibition and a publication of a companion book required the assistance and commitment of many individuals, organizations, and institutions. We are indebted first and foremost to Don Nakanishi, director of the UCLA Asian American Studies Center, who generously supported the project. We would also like to thank his staff: Angeline Camandang, Cathy Castor, Kay Dumlao, Teresa Ejanda, Mary Kao, Princeton Kim, Marji Lee, Russell Leong, Meg Thornton, and Christine Wang.

Within the UCLA academic community, we would like to acknowledge the following individuals: Jose Garcia, Roy Hamilton, Stacey Hong, David Mayo, Betsy Quick, Kristen Quine, Lisa Rosen, Doran Ross, and Christine Sellin for graciously hosting the photograph exhibition at the Fowler Museum of Cultural History; Albert Boime, David Kunzle, and Donald Preziosi of the Department of Art History for providing thoughtful advice and insightful comments on the theoretical and practical concerns relating to the exhibition; undergraduate students Cristina Espiritu and Maryann Szyskowski of the Student

Research Program for assisting us in the documentation phase; and the staff at the Visual Resource Collection and Office of Instructional Development for processing large volumes of slide orders on short notice.

While this project gave us the opportunity to rekindle old relations and establish new ones, our *utang na loob* goes also to the members of the Filipino-American community organizations in the West coast who offered their invaluable support. They include Jerome Academia, who originally suggested the idea of mounting a photograph exhibition, and Jilly Canizares of the Festival of Philippine Arts and Culture; Joel Jacinto of Search to Involve Pilipino Americans for initiating the first meeting of what would later become the Photograph Exhibit Committee; Abraham Ferrer, whose artistic prowess gave our gallery brochures and this book the professional 'look and feel', and Linda Mabalot of Visual Communications; Dorothy and Fred Cordova and Sam Balucas and Emily Lawsin (L.A. Chapter) of the Filipino American National Historical Society; and Tania Azores of the Pilipino American Reading Room and Library.

The hardest task of the exhibition phase was searching for photographs. The people who supplied contact, caption, and/or copyright information include Xavier Aboitiz, Tom Featherstone of the Archives of Urban and Labor Affairs at Wayne State University, Annalissa Herbert, Abe Ignacio (also for giving us access to his personal collection of magazines, newspapers, and books), Ira Jacknis of the Phoebe Hearst Museum of Anthropology at UC Berkeley, Clare Salaveria, Steffi San Buenaventura, Helen Toribio of City College of San Francisco, and Jim Zwick of Syracuse University. Ria Bagaybagayan and Agnes Bertiz of the University of Southern California, Reuben Domingo of Puro Arte Gallery and Performance Space, Irene Soriano of Babaye Productions, and *Filipinas Magazine* also assisted us. At various stages of the exhibition and publication, overseas support became necessary. We would like to thank Fruto Corre of the Film Center and Patrick Flores of the Department of Art Studies at the University of the Philippines-Diliman (Philippines), Alya Honasan of Metro Guide Publications (Philippines), and Ana Labrador of Cambridge University (United Kingdom) who instantly became international 'people finders', providing 'white-page service' to us free of charge.

Permission to use the photographs shown in the exhibition and those published herein were granted by the de la Cruz Family, Ejanda Family, Editions Didier Millet Pte Ltd (Singapore), Jonathan Best Private Collection, Katipunan ng Demokratikong Pilipino Oakland, CA), Library of Congress (Washington, DC), Lyndon B. Johnson Library (Austin, TX), Eduardo Masferré Souvenirs (Orange, NJ), McFarland Publishing & Co. (Jefferson, NC), National Archives (Washington, DC), Paul Ashton Private Collection, Philippine Resource Center (Berkeley, CA), Saint Louis Public Library (St. Louis, MO), *San Francisco Examiner* (San Francisco, CA), Take Stock, Images of Change (San Rafael, CA), The Bettmann Archive (New York, NY), The Filipino American National Historical Society (Seattle, WA), The James Reuter Foundation (Philippines), The Missouri Historical Society (St. Louis, MO), University of Oklahoma Press (Tulsa, OK), Visual Communications (Los Angeles, CA), and Xavier Aboitiz Private Collection.

The photographers who shared their work with us and whom we had great pleasure of meeting either through e-mail, telephone, or in person were George Ballis (Oakland, CA), Imelda Cajipe-Endaya (Philippines), Cirilo Domine (Los Angeles, CA), Lillian Galedo (Berkeley, CA), Catherine Karnow (San Francisco, CA), Kim Komenich (San Francisco, CA), Lenny Limjoco (San Francisco, CA), Oliver Nan Mateo (Los Angeles, CA), Rick Rocamora (San Francisco, CA), Frans Welman (The Netherlands), and Roberto Yñiguez (Philippines).

Another major aspect of the photograph exhibition is the "Evidence and Encounter: Film and Lecture Series". This public program is screening *Bontoc Eulogy* (1995) by Marlon Fuentes, *A Filipino in America* (1938) by Doroteo Ines, *Sakay* (1993) by Raymond Red, and *Orapronobis* (1990) by Lino Brocka. Guest lecturers providing film commentary and/or historical background include independent filmmaker Marlon Fuentes, Geoffrey Robinson and Michael Salman of the UCLA History Department, and Steffi San Buenaventura of the UC Riverside Ethnic Studies Department. We thank them all.

This book, however, *is* the icing on the cake. Who would have imagined that an afternoon conversation with Geoffrey Robinson would save our dream and, ultimately, lead to the publication of a companion book to the photograph exhibition? His enthusiasm and belief in the importance of the project are unparalleled, and we thank him, Judy Mitoma, and the rest of those involved with the UCLA Southeast Asia Program wholeheartedly.

Indeed, the journey has been long, yet fruitful. We hope the photograph exhibition will have the opportunity to travel to other university art museums and community centers so that others can get a glimpse of the complexity of Philippine and U.S. relations. Finally, we express our deepest gratitude to the familiar folks and new acquaintances who joined us during the special opening event of the photograph exhibition on August 23, 1998. We share this book with you.

The Curators—
Pearlie Rose S. Baluyut
Enrique B. de la Cruz
Rico J. Reyes

CONFRONTATIONS, CROSSINGS, AND CONVERGENCE:
Photographs of the Philippines and the United States, 1898-1998

1998 marks the centennial of three historic occasions: the end of Spanish colonialism, the proclamation of the Philippine Republic, and the advent of American rule. As a way of exploring the complex and long-standing relationship of the Philippines and the United States, the exhibition and book retrospectively capture the last century through the medium of photography.

Rather than merely present photographs in their conventional form as *evidence* of history, photography is redefined as an *encounter*—both moment and site of power in the narration and representation of Philippine-U.S. history. Power, however, must be understood not simply as a relationship of domination and resistance, but also that where nuanced negotiation occurs. As the exhibition and book investigate the power of pictures, notions of identity and culture are complicated, colonial and nationalist histories are reframed, and boundaries of modern states are reconfigured.

The prints are drawn from a wide range of sources, including governmental archives, libraries, museums, and personal collections in Asia, Europe, and North America, and are organized under four overlapping themes. Staged as isolated moments or a recurring series, these monumental and fragmentary images offer disorienting flashbacks and multiple perspectives that problematize our reading of Philippine-U.S. history. Orchestrated as a visual ensemble that traces the glimmers of the past into the present and vice versa, they run counter to the theory that a blink of the camera's eye freezes time.

As a centennial reflection, the exhibition and the book crystallize the manifold confrontations between the Philippines and the United States, the endless crossings of peoples, commodities, and culture, and the complex convergence of motives, desires, and vision. More importantly, they stand as evidence of shifting power relations *and* encounters with domination, resistance, and negotiation.

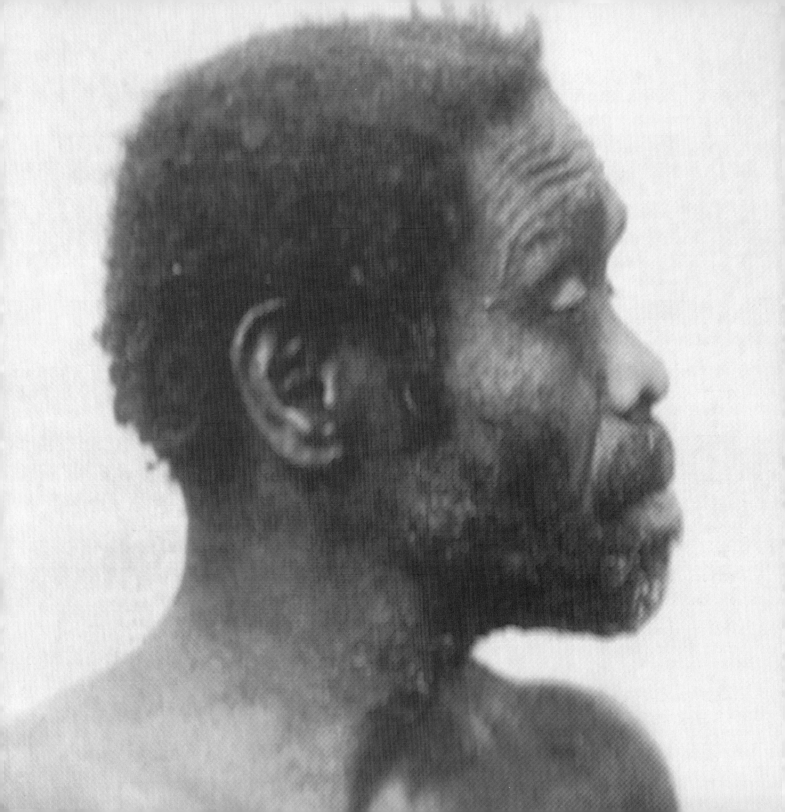

SPECTACLE AND SURVEILLANCE

The Spanish-American War culminated in the United States' annexation of colonies in the Caribbean and the Pacific in 1898. Despite widespread resistance to the new empire and its policies, American diplomatic representatives and scholars proceeded to assess the present and discuss the future of the people of the Philippines.

As part of the United States' programmatic mobilization of public opinion and sentiment at home to support its colonial scaffolding abroad, an ideological warfare was waged through visual propaganda. Ocular proofs that scientifically demonstrated the racial predicament of the Filipinos were manufactured. Then described as the 'little brown brothers' only capable of aping the Americans, their bodies were measured, disciplined, and displayed. The images assembled under this theme illustrate how the Americans dealt with their fascination and fear of the Filipinos—the new burden of the White Man.

The Louisiana Purchase Exposition in St. Louis in 1904 stands as a paradigm for the many encounters engineered by the United States to justify its prolonged tutelage of the Filipinos. The ethnographic displays of the "miniature, the gigantic, and the bizarre" the world had ever seen transformed the exposition into a breathtaking spectacle. But if spectacle, according to art theorist W.J.T. Mitchell, "is the ideological form of pictorial power, surveillance is its bureaucratic, managerial, and disciplinary form." Infrastructures such as prisons and schools, which bore punitive and reformative tasks, became instruments of colonization and civilization that transformed the Filipinos into law-abiding citizens.

Through the United States' love affair with science which gave birth to representations of so-called 'truth' and 'progress' or the lack thereof, the choreographed encounters between the spectator-surveyor (the Americans) and the spectacle-surveyed (the Filipinos) were realized. As advocates of both expansionism and anti-imperialism in the United States debated over their country's involvement in the Philippines, the mass (re)production of the Filipino as the Other was sustained by photography. Participating actively in the discourse of colonialism, this medium advertised the power of the emerging American empire.

A Meeting of the Philippine Commission in Washington, D.C. (L-R: Honorable Jacob Gould Shurman, President of Cornell University; Honorable Charles Denby, Former U.S. Minister to China; Professor Dean Conant Worcester, University of Michigan; and Admiral George Dewey)

Washington, D.C., November 1899
Robert Melville
Mario Wilcox, *Harper's History of the War in the Philippines* (New York: Harper & Brothers Publishers, 1900)
[Reprinted in Manila: Vera Reyes, Inc., 1979].

"IT IS SAID that when John D. Long, Secretary of the Navy in President McKinley's cabinet, received the news of the battle of Manila Bay, he at once turned to an atlas to find out where Manila was. From the battle dates the active interest of Americans in a remote and hitherto unconsidered archipelago—an interest which brought about not a colonial government, for America never colonized the Philippines, but a trusteeship in government until the islanders became able to administer their own affairs. The success of this trusteeship was wholly due to the character of the [twelve] men sent out from the United States to supervise the unwanted and unwilling wards for whom a strange turn of events had made our government responsible."

—Arthur S. Pier, Author of *American Apostles to the Philippines*

GEORGE DEWEY
..."whose destruction of the Spanish fleet led to America's occupation of the Philippine Islands."

FREDERICK FUNSTON
..."who ended the organized Philippine Insurrection by capturing General [Emilio] Aguinaldo."

WILLIAM HOWARD TAFT
..."who established civil government and initiated the era of good will between Americans and Filipinos."

LUKE EDWARD WRIGHT
..."who ran the threads of order and organization through the structure of the government."

LEONARD WOOD
..."who restored decency and credit to the Philippine government after a period of misrule."

DEAN CONANT WORCESTER
..."who encouraged science and brought peace and fair dealing to the savages of the interior."

Credits, all photos on this page and next:
location and specific dates unknown
Anonymous
Arthur S. Pier,
American Apostles to the Philippines (Boston: The Beacon Press, 1950).

FRANK WATSON CARPENTER
…"who taught the Filipino rulers of provinces and cities the American ethical principles of government."

WARWICK GREENE
…"who organized the governmental engineering forces, and taught Filipinos how to build and maintain their roads."

JOHN SYLVANUS LEECH
…"who made the Bureau of Printing a technical school in which the Filipinos could learn to become self-respecting and self-supporting artisans."

JOHN JOSEPH PERSHING
…"whose masterly campaign against the previously uncontrolled Moros led to later high command which made him potent in world history."

RICHARD PEARSON STRONG
…"whose researches into the causes and cure of tropical disease won for him leadership in his field."

CHARLES HENRY BRENT
…"who, as first Episcopal Bishop of the Philippines, inspired all who knew him by his high ethical standards; and who conducted an international campaign against the evils of narcotics."

Igorot Boy With Camera: One Among the Many People from Different Ethnic Groups in the Philippines Brought to the 1904 St. Louis Exposition

St. Louis Exposition, St. Louis, Missouri, 1904
Anonymous (attri. Jessie Tarbox Beals)
Special Collections, St. Louis Public Library, St. Louis, MO (RB-F)

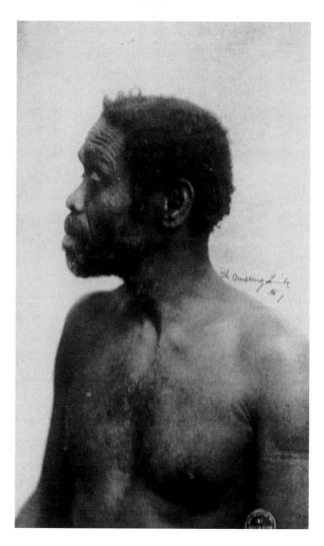

"The Negritos, according to various official descriptions of their village, were 'extremely low in intellect,' and 'it is believed that they will eventually become extinct.'"
—Robert W. Rydell, *All the World's a Fair*

St. Louis Exposition, St. Louis, Missouri, 1904
The Gerhard Sisters
Library of Congress, Washington, D.C. (LC-U5Z62-102927)

Two photographs of a Bontoc Igorot Boy, With the Second Taken Nine Years After the First

Philippines, 1904 and 1913
Anonymous (attri. Dean Worcester)
Dean Worcester, *The Philippines Past and Present*. Vol. 2 (New York: Macmillan Company, 1914).

Entrance to the Quiangan School-House With Two Ifugao Boys on Either Side of the Stairway. Similar to the Gorgons in the pediments of ancient temples or the lion statues outside modern Western libraries, the boys by virtue of their 'ifugaoness' functioned apotropaeically—as symbolic guardians of the school from intruders, vandals, and/or bad spirits.

Quiangan, Mountain Province, Philippines, ca. 1913
Anonymous
Dean Worcester, *The Philippines Past and Present.* Vol. 2
(New York: Macmillan Company, 1914).

To silence critics of U.S. involvement in the Philippines, and as testimony to America's civilizing mission, "model" schoolhouses in the Philippines were often recorded or put on display.

"Wednesday: Be Kind, Just, and Merciful"

Manila, Philippines, ca. 1900s
Anonymous
The Bettmann Archive, New York, NY

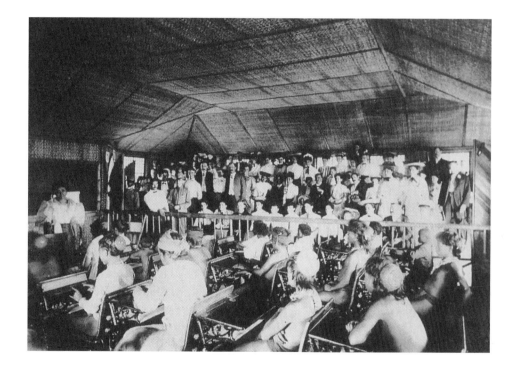

Fairgoers Visiting a Model School in the 'Philippine Reservation' at the St. Louis Exposition

St. Louis Exposition, St. Louis, Missouri, 1904
Anonymous
National Archives, Washington, D.C. (43-EX-2N-17)

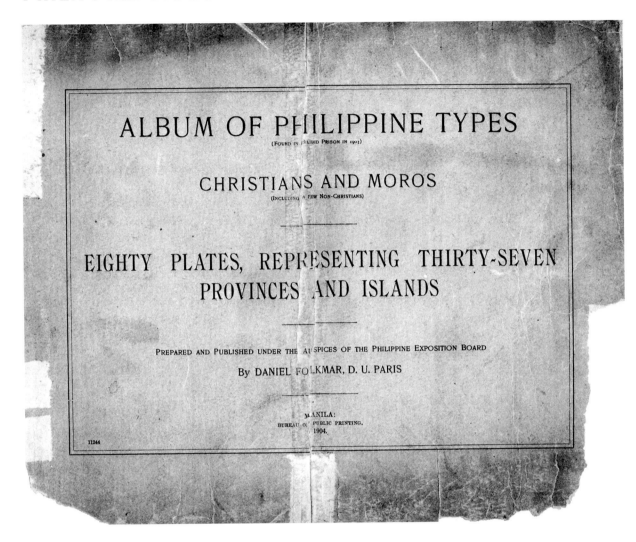

Daniel Folkmar, *Album of Philippine Types* (*Found in Bilibid Prison in 1903*), *Christians and Moros* (*Including a Few Non-Christians*), *Eighty Plates, Representing Thirty-Seven Provinces and Islands* (Manila: Bureau of Public Printing, 1904).

Seen as a whole, the seriality of the images, the anonymity of the prisoners, and the accompanying charts of physical measurements suggest how the entire population of the archipelago was cast as the 'criminal type' of civilization to be incarcerated and reformed.

Book (frontispiece), plus next three pages

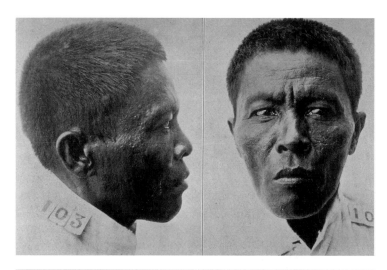

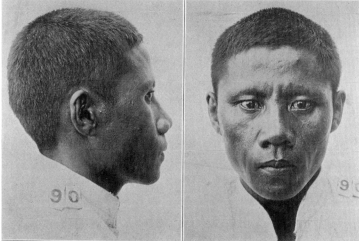

**TOP: Photograph No. 103: A Bicol of Ambos Camarines Province
(Age 31, Bilibid Prison No. 29 C)**

**BOTTOM: Photograph No. 90: An Ilocano of Ilocos Norte Province
(Age 27, Bilibid Prison No. 1311 P)**

Manila, Philippines, 1903
Anonymous

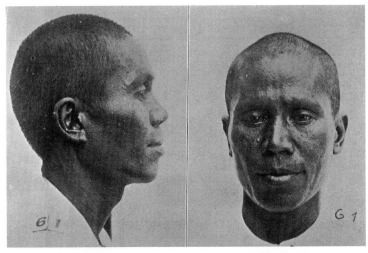

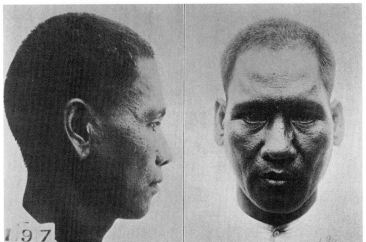

**TOP: Photograph No. 61: A Moro of Cottabato [sic] Subprovince
(Age 40, Bilibid Prison No. 1585 P),**

**BOTTOM: Photograph No. 197: A Macabebe of Pampanga Province
(Age 36, Bilibid Prison No. 1538 P)**

Manila, Philippines, 1903
Anonymous

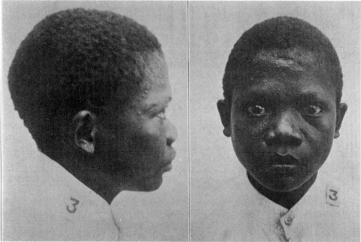

TOP: Photograph No. 220: A Zambal of Zambales Province
(Age 39, Bilibid Prison No. 1674 P)

BOTTOM: Photograph No. 3: A Negrito of Bataan Province
(Age 15, Bilibid Prison No. 2339 C)

Manila, Philippines, 1903
Anonymous

DIASPORA, STRUGGLES, AND SURVIVAL

Between 1565 and 1811, Spanish galleons carrying trade goods and human cargo shuttled from the ports of Manila and Acapulco. Some Filipino sailors who were drafted into maritime service by the Spaniards found their way into Louisiana, while others joined Spanish expeditions into California. Significant Filipino migration into the United States began, however, under the American empire.

In the early decades of the twentieth century, U.S. government-sponsored Filipino students arrived to be schooled in American civilization. These *pensionados* were later followed by contract laborers in Hawaiian plantations and California farms. Recruited primarily as single men, they came to be seen as a racial threat to the white community. Like the Chinese and Japanese before them who endured the Oriental Exclusion Act in the nineteenth century, the Filipinos suffered from racial exclusion, cultural isolation, and legalized anti-miscegenation which prevented a majority of them from starting families and establishing communities.

Despite anti-Filipino sentiment and legal restrictions, new relationships emerged. In taxi-dance halls, for example, the Filipinos and poor white immigrant women forged social alliances to overcome racial, class, and gender oppression. As mixed marriages and continued labor migration increased their numbers, Filipinos established self-help groups patterned after Masonic organizations, athletic clubs, and labor unions. Interestingly, Americans formed similar systems of support while stationed in the Philippines. With the Philippine Independence Act of 1934, however, Filipino migration to the United States was drastically reduced. It was not until the end of World War II that the annual immigration quota of fifty was lifted, allowing the Filipinos who served in the war to bring their Filipina "war brides" to the United States.

The Filipinos' voyage eastward across the Pacific continues to this day. Despite unfavorable winds and an unfamiliar and often hostile terrain, the Filipinos are learning, like their predecessors aboard the galleons, to navigate through America. As they leave the archipelago and adopt a new homeland, they become transnational. Their photographs confirm the empowerment of a new body politic, the Filipino Americans.

The self-given name of this group of U.S. government-sponsored students or *pensionados* who arrived in Seattle on the S.S. President Jefferson. L-R: (kneeling) Dr. Patrocino Valenzuela and Atty. Rufino Luna; (first row, standing) Dr. Vicente R. Sayo, Ramon Racelia, Maria Villa, Francisco T. Roque, Feliza Calderon, Jesus Alvarez, Simeon Mangaliman, and Dr. Mariano Basaca; (sitting on rail) Alejandro de Mesa, Andres Borromeo, Macario Naval, Alexander Gordon, Mamerto Cruz, and Tomas Abello.

Seattle, Washington, 7 September 1924
Anonymous
Fred Cordova, *Filipinos: Forgotten Asian Americans: A Pictorial Essay, 1763-circa 1963* (Dubuque: Kendall/Hunt Publishing, 1983).

Stockton, California, ca. 1930s
Anonymous
Visual Communications, Los Angeles, CA (FA0038)

Filipino American Lettuce Pickers During the Great Depression

Imperial Valley, California, ca. 1935-1938
Dorothea Lange
Library of Congress, Washington, D.C. (LC-U5Z62-19804)

Division I, Lodge I: To overcome racial and cultural isolation, early Filipino immigrants formed self-help organizations.

location unknown, April 1926
Anonymous
Lorenzo de los Reyes, *Every Day New and Wonder* (Lorenzo de los Reyes, 1931). [Courtesy of Steffi San Buenaventura]

Filipinos in Western Suit

Stockton, California, ca. 1920s-1930s
Anonymous
Visual Communications, Los Angeles, CA

**In Search of Suitors: The Bilar Sisters in Filipino Terno
(Now Feling Darangan and Catherine Autentico)**

Stockton, California, 1929
Anonymous
Visual Communications, Los Angeles, CA

Wedding in Las Vegas, Nevada. To circumvent anti-miscegenation laws in California, Filipino men and their American brides often crossed statelines to get married.

Las Vegas, Nevada, 1953
Anonymous
Visual Communications, Los Angeles, CA (PA0015)

WAYS OF BELONGING

Relying instead on sports to establish a sense of community, athletic clubs provided the necessary support to the youth in the Philippines and in the United States.

Major Brown's Brownies: An American Little League in the Philippines

Manila, Philippines, 1903
Anonymous
Xavier Aboitiz Private Collection

Pilipino Basketball Club in America

Los Angeles, California, 1928
Anonymous
Visual Communications, Los Angeles, CA (FA0025)

Mrs. Frank Mancao and Daughters with Unidentified Farm Laborers. The gender imbalance that existed between Filipino men and women who came to the United States made it difficult for immigrants to start families. Although women were clearly outnumbered, they acquired the powerful role of a matriarch, a pillar of strength at home and in the community.

Reedley, California, ca. 1930
Frank A. Mancao
Fred Cordova, *Filipinos: Forgotten Asian Americans: A Pictorial Essay*, 1763-circa 1963 (Dubuque: Kendall/Hunt Publishing, 1983).

President Lyndon B. Johnson Signs the Immigration Act of 1965 on New York's Liberty Island. With him are Vice-President Hubert Humphrey (front, third from left) and Attorney General Robert Kennedy (front, second from right). This legislation finally eliminated race-based quotas as a feature of U.S. Immigration policy, opening America's door to all people, including the Filipinos.

Ellis Island, New York, 1965
Anonymous
President Lyndon B. Johnson Library, Austin, TX

'Illegitimate' Desires: Widespread fear of 'racial contamination' led to prohibitions against Filipinos. Nonetheless, Filipino men and American women discovered creative ways to cross the barriers.

Mrs. Wilkins Teaching an Igorot the Cakewalk

St. Louis Exposition, St. Louis, Missouri, 1904
Charles Martin
The Missouri Historical Society, St. Louis, MO (A- 9/P-11)

An American Taxi Dancer and Her Filipino Escort Outside a Dance Hall

location unknown, ca. 1920s-1930s
Anonymous
Visual Communications, Los Angeles, CA

In the 1970s, farm workers were able to obtain land in Delano, California, on which to build retirement housing for aging Filipino farm workers. During its construction, hundreds of Filipinos from the San Francisco Bay area and Los Angeles traveled to Delano on weekends to provide volunteer labor for the project. The project was named Agbayani Village, after Paolo Agbayani, a Filipino farmworker who died on the picket lines during the Grape Pickers' Strike in 1967.

Filipino carpenter Chris Braga supervised volunteers during the construction of Agbayani Village.

California, 1976
Anonymous
Visual Communications, Los Angeles, CA

"Agbayani Village: Coming Soon"

Delano, California, 1976
Anonymous
Visual Communications, Los Angeles, CA

RESISTANCE AND COLLABORATION

The first two wars that the United States fought in Asia in this century—the Philippine-American War and the Second World War—epitomized the height of resistance and collaboration between Filipinos and Americans. The former, where a million Filipinos were estimated to have died as they were being "rescued" by 250,000 American troops from the Spaniards, was often referred to as the "Philippine Insurrection", completely ignoring Filipino aspirations for independence. To molify American opposition, the war was declared over in July 1902, yet fighting continued well into the first decade of the century.

Almost half a century later, another war would visit the archipelago. With the surprise Japanese attack on Pearl Harbor in 1941, America's war with the Rising Sun transformed the Philippines into a war zone once more. At home and abroad, the United States drafted Filipinos and Americans to either fight the Japanese in exchange for citizenship and/or benefits or provide medical assistance. United in surrender, in the Death March, and in concentration camps, this war symbolized Philippine-U.S. fraternity. The Filipinos who served in the United States Forces in the Far East (USAFFE) emerged as heroes and patriots, giving those in the United States a measure of dignity and self respect.

Unlike the Philippine-American War, the image of Americans changed from conquerors to liberators during the Second World War. Yet for all its 'good' intentions, the United States rescued the Philippines from the Japanese Imperial Forces by bombing it, giving Manila the distinction of being the most heavily destroyed city in Asia and the Pacific. Pictures of architectural ruins, mass starvation, and death, bear witness to the war, yet no photographic trace of the sufferings of the comfort women existed.

The second World War and its aftermath remain a tale of calculated betrayal. In exchange for Philippine independence in 1946, the United States government declared that the Filipinos who fought during World War II were ineligible for veteran benefits. To the aging Filipino American veterans, General Douglas MacArthur never fulfilled his promise to return. Imprisoned by time and longing for status recognition, they form a battalion of resistance today that challenges the policies in Washington.

Revolutionary Leaders Exiled in Hong Kong

Hong Kong, 1898
Anonymous
Mario Wilcox, *Harper's History of the War in the Philippines* (New York: Harper & Brothers Publishers, 1900)
[Reprinted in Manila: Vera Reyes, Inc., 1979].

Moro Massacre at Mount Dajo: For a brief moment in 1906, news of the massacre of 900 Muslim Filipinos—men, women, and children—on the southern Philippine island of Jolo brought the war in the Philippines onto the front pages of newspapers across the United States, eliciting this poignant remark from Moorefield Storey, President of the U.S. Anti-Imperialist League, "[T]he spirit which slaughters brown men in Jolo is the same spirit which lynches black men in the South."

Mount Dajo, Jolo, Philippines, 9 March 1906
Anonymous
National Archives, Washington, D.C. (111-SC-83648)

-1898-
TO THOSE WHO
VOLUNTEERED AND
EXTENDED THE HAND
OF LIBERTY TO
ALIEN PEOPLES
-1902-
ERECTED 1950 BY
UNITED SPANISH
WAR VETERANS

LOUIS LEONARD McCLARY
CHAIRMAN

ROGER NOBLE BURNHAM
SCULPTURE

Monument to Whom? The Philippine-American War as the Spanish-American War.

Los Angeles National Cemetery, Westwood, California, 1998
Enrique de la Cruz
Courtesy of the de la Cruz Family

Gregorio del Pilar   **Isidro Torres**   **Artemio Ricarte**   **Tomas Mascardo**   **Gen. Emilio Aguinaldo**

During the Spanish-American War of 1898, Americans sought the collaboration of Filipino revolutionary leaders.

Credits for all photos on this spread:
Philippines, ca. 1898
Anonymous
Mario Wilcox, *Harper's History of the War in the Philippines* (New York: Harper & Brothers Publishers, 1900) [Reprinted in Manila: Vera Reyes, Inc., 1979].

Jose Ignacio Paua   **Pantaleon Garcia**   **Brig. Gen. Cardeñas**   **Francisco Prieto**   **Antonio Luna**

"General Emilio Aguinaldo, with Director of Education Frank L. Crone...[standing] beside a field of corn planted by Emilio Aguinaldo, Jr., in a school contest, typifies the peace, prosperity, and enlightenment which have been brought about in the Philippine Islands under American rule."

Philippines, ca. 1913
Anonymous
Dean Worcester, *The Philippines Past and Present*. Vol. 1 (New York: Macmillan Company, 1914).

Admiral George Dewey and Officers of His Squadron, Aboard His Flagship, the *Olympia*

Manila Bay, Philippines, 1898
J.C. Hemment
George Dewey, *Autobiography of George Dewey, Admiral of the Navy*
(New York: Charles Scribner's Sons, 1916).

Between 1920 and 1934, the Philippines sent several missions to the United States to lobby for Philippine Independence. The mission headed by Manuel L. Quezon (center) returns from the United States with the Tydings-McDuffie Act, giving commonwealth status to the Philippines and promising independence in 10 years.

Manila, Philippines, 1934
Anonymous
Ferdinand E. Marcos (attri.),
Kasaysayan: History of the Filipinos
(Manila: Pambansang Sentro sa Kabatirang Madla at Paglalathala, 1970).

Filipino and American troops outside the 1,400-foot Malinta Tunnel in Corregidor, where their garrison withstood 27 days of artillery bombardment.

Corregidor, Philippines, ca. 1942
Tsuguichi Koyomagi
WWII: Time-Life Books History of the Second World War (New York: Prentice Hall Press, 1989)

Mila Calma: A 22-Year-Old Guerrilla Holds Aloft the Banner of the Filipino Resistance. With the retreat of General Douglas MacArthur to Australia and the surrender of Filipino and American forces under USAFFE to the Japanese Imperial Forces, Filipinos engaged in guerrilla warfare against the Japanese.

Philippines, 1945
Anonymous
National Archives, Washington, D.C.

Bataan Nurses Outside Nurses Quarters Tent at Hospital No. 2 (L-R: Lieutenant Josephine Nesbitt, Captain M.C. Davison, and Lieutenant Helen Hennessey)

Bataan, Philippines, ca. 1940s
Anonymous
Donald J. Young, *The Battle of Bataan: A History of the 90 Day Siege and Eventual Surrender of 75,000 Filipinos and United States Troops to the Japanese in World War II* (Jefferson, North Carolina: McFarland and Company, Inc., 1992).

Mary Abastilla Beltran Posing with A Friend Before Joining the American Red Cross in the United States

Philippines, ca. 1930s-1940s
Anonymous
Fred Cordova, *Filipinos: Forgotten Asian Americans: A Pictorial Essay, 1763-circa 1963*
(Dubuque: Kendall/Hunt Publishing, 1983).

Mass Naturalization Ceremony of the First Filipino Infantry Regiment (U.S. Army) Who Chose to Become American Citizens

Camp Beale, California, 1943
Anonymous
Fred Cordova, *Filipinos: Forgotten Asian Americans: A Pictorial Essay, 1763-circa 1963* (Dubuque: Kendall/Hunt Publishing, 1983).

Graduating Class of U.S. Navy Stewards. After the Second World War, enlisting in the U.S. Navy gave Filipinos the opportunity to migrate to the United States. Recruited through U.S. bases in the Philippines, most Filipinos served as stewards to American naval officers during their tour of duty.

U.S.N.T.C., San Diego, California, 8 December 1967
Anonymous
Courtesy of the Ejanda Family

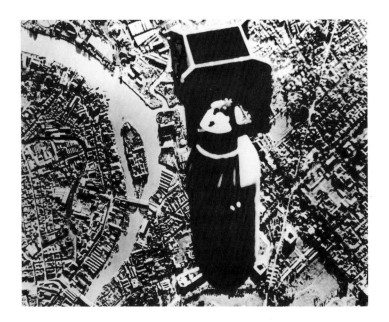

A 2000-Pound American Bomb Is Dropped on Manila

Manila, Philippines, 22 November 1944
Anonymous (attri. U.S. Air Force Photographer)
National Archives, Washington, D.C. (80G-272604)

TOP: The First Landing of General Douglas MacArthur

Leyte, Philippines, 20 October 1944
Major Gaetano Faillace
National Archives, Washington, D.C.

RIGHT: MacArthur Park War Memorial: A Time of 'Cleansing' for the 50th Anniversary of the Liberation of the Philippines (bronze sculpture based on Carl Mydans' photograph).

Leyte, Philippines, 1994
Reuters News Service
The Bettmann Archive, New York, N.Y.

A Half-Starved Filipino Child Hangs Tightly to Her Ration Box while Manila Burns in the Background

Manila, Philippines, 7 February 1945
Major Gaetano Faillace
National Archives, Washington, D.C. (SC-203030)

LEFT: American Tank Enters Fort Santiago

Manila, Philippines, 26 February 1945
Anonymous
National Archives, Washington, D.C. (80G-273361)

RIGHT: Plaza de España, Intramuros (Walled City)

Manila, Philippines, 23 February 1945
Anonymous
National Archives, Washington, D.C. (80G-273409)

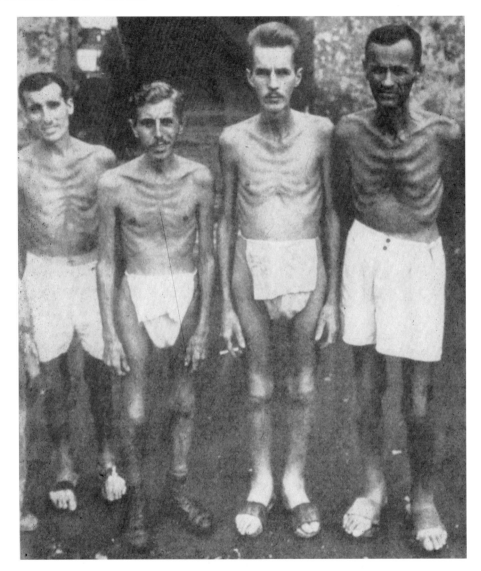

Condition of the Prisoners after Their Release from Bilibid Prison (L-R: Sid Roberts, a Scotsman; Whipps, a Londoner; Jim Ballard, a special prisoner; and U.S. Sergeant I.E. Raum, a tuberculosis patient)

Manila, Philippines, 4 February 1945
Anonymous (attri. to a U.S. Navy Photographer of Prisoners)
William A. Berry (with James Edwin Alexander), *Prisoner of the Rising Sun* (Norman: University of Oklahoma, 1993).

Then and Now: Filipino Veteran Sergio Quinal Holds A Portrait of Himself in Uniform at Age 21. Thousands of Filipino WWII veterans who fought under USAFFE live in poverty and are now fighting for veteran benefits that were denied them soon after WWII ended.

San Francisco, California, ca. 1990s
Rick Rocamora
Courtesy of the Artist

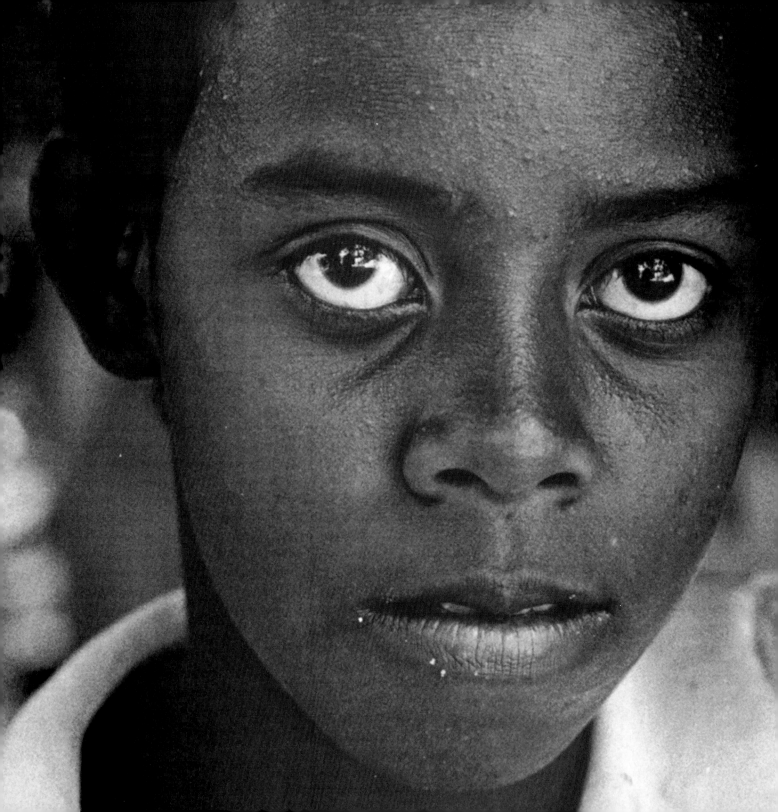

CLOSURES, FRACTURES, AND PARALLELS

On the 4th of July in 1946, the Philippines became politically independent from the United States. Nevertheless, the United States continued to influence Philippine policies, while corporations exploited its natural resources and labor. As visual coda, the photographs assembled under this theme reprise the complex episodes in Philippine-U.S. history.

In the prevailing Cold War atmosphere, the United States condoned Ferdinand Marcos' dictatorship (1965-1986) and ignored its gruesome record of human rights violations. A vibrant opposition movement developed in both hemispheres, composed by Filipinos and Americans alike. The popular revolution that became an international symbol of people power finally tore away any pretense of democracy, forcing the White House to move Marcos to a life of exile in Hawaii.

The removal of U.S. military bases in 1992 eliminated the last vestiges of colonial rule over the archipelago, yet the imprint of American empire in the Philippines remains visible. Below the U.S.-owned corporate skyscrapers and evening skyline of neon advertisements, its legacy looms over the streets plastered with Hollywood-inspired billboards and congested with remodeled World War II jeepneys. The most important, yet often neglected reminder of the relationship of the Philippines and the United States are the Amerasians, abandoned children of American G.I.s with Filipinas who worked near the bases.

From this centennial vantage point, we gaze through a rear window. Embracing the stereotypes and ideals circulated in the past and the realities and improvisations offered by the present, these photographs revisit the multiple moments and sites of power struggles. The century-long journey of the Filipinos and the Americans has been a process of discovery and becoming for both and the future is sure to bring further encounters of domination, resistance, and negotiation.

Pumipiglas **(Struggling): Prisoners of Conscience. Oppositionists to the authoritarian regime of Ferdinand Marcos were often arrested and jailed without due process.**

Bahbah, Agusan del Sur Provincial Prison, Philippines, 1980
Lenny Limjoco
Courtesy of the Artist

LEFT: Protecting the Vote: The dictator Ferdinand Marcos held a presidential snap elections in February 1986 to prove a boast. The unprecedented voter turnout in support of the opposition candidate Corazon Aquino precipitated his downfall. When the polls closed, pollwatchers often resorted to physically protecting the ballot boxes from tampering.

Manila, Philippines, February 1986
Robert Gumpert
Philippine Resource Center, Berkeley, CA (8633-18A)

RIGHT: Fearless Front-Liners Block Marcos Loyalist Forces Outside Camp Aguinaldo along EDSA (Epifanio de los Santos Avenue)

Quezon City, Philippines, February 1986
Kim Komenich
San Francisco Examiner, San Francisco, CA

Larry Dulay Itliong (front, left) and Cesar Chavez (front, right) Lead the United Farm Workers in their Strike Against California's Grape Growers With Walter Reuther (front, center), President of United Auto Workers, Pledging His Support

California, 1965
George Ballis
Take Stock, Images of Change, San Rafael, CA

Picket signs protesting the eviction of elderly Filipino and Chinese from the International Hotel, one of the few establishments providing affordable housing for Senior Citizens near San Francisco's Chinatown. Owners of the hotel sought the eviction of tenants to redevelop the land. After several years of protest, the owners succeeded in evicting the tenants and razing the building, but to this day, the site of the I-Hotel remains undeveloped.

San Francisco, California, 1974
Larry Fong
Visual Communications, Los Angeles, CA (PC0070/72)

Members of the Union of Democratic Filipinos (KDP) Protest the Murders of Cannery Union Organizers Silme Domingo and Gene Viernes

Seattle, Washington, 3 June 1981
John Stamets
Katipunan ng Demokratikong Pilipino (KDP) Collection, Oakland, CA

"Oppose U.S. Support for the Marcos Dictatorship!" When Ferdinand Marcos declared Martial Law in September 1972, he relied on U.S. support to maintain his political hegemony. Almost overnight, a strong opposition movement was established by Filipino Americans.

San Francisco, California, ca. 1980s
Rick Rocamora
Courtesy of the Artist

"Marcos Flees," Leaving His Monumental Bust in the Background Unfinished. "Throughout his public career...[Ferdinand Marcos portrayed] a greater-than-life image of himself...[and] could never be content with what he was or what he had...Marcos could not just be a brilliant student—he had to be the best. He could not just be a war hero—he had to be the most decorated hero ever. He could not just be a politician—he had to be the president of the Philippines. Nor could he simply be President—he had to be dictator for life."
—Carmen Navarro Pedrosa, Author of *Imelda Marcos*

Tuba, Mountain Province, Philippines, 26 February 1986
Roberto Yñiguez
Courtesy of the Artist

Cory and the Pink Nuns in a Carmelite Convent

Quezon City, Philippines, February 1986
Catherine Karnow
Editions Didier Millet, Singapore

The Seduction of Hollywood and the Chaos of World War II

Manila, Philippines, October 1995
Paul Chesley
Editions Didier Millet, Singapore

The Busy Escolta by Day

Escolta, Philippines, ca. 1900s
Anonymous
Xavier Aboitiz Private Collection

Signs of Capital in EDSA (Epifanio de los Santos Avenue) at Night

Mandaluyong, Metro Manila, Philippines, October 1995
Catherine Karnow
Editions Didier Millet, Singapore

American Junk From Military Base. In 1992, the Philippine Senate refused to renew the treaty that enabled the United States to maintain strategic military bases on Philippine soil.

Philippines, 1991
Frans Welman
Courtesy of the Artist

An Amerasian Living Outside Subic Naval Base

Olongapo, Zambales, Philippines, ca. 1990s
Rick Rocamora
Courtesy of the Artist

Filipina: DH (Domestic Helper) (Detail of installation with found objects, plaster-bonded textiles, projected images, text, and sound). Stereotypes have genealogies. As early as the turn of the century, Filipinas, like the mammies in U.S. southern plantations, were employed by American families stationed in the Philippines to care for their children.

Manila, Philippines, 1995 (projected photograph, ca. 1900s)
Imelda Cajipe-Endaya
Courtesy of the Artist

Rear Window (Detail of an installation entitled _Salon derrière, ca. 1933_) Early Filipino immigrants in the 1920s-1930s portrayed their masculinity to assimilate to American culture; some Filipino Americans today are redefining 'masculinity' to create a sense of belonging.

Los Angeles, California, 1996
Rico J. Reyes, Cirilo Domine, and Oliver Nan Mateo
Courtesy of the Artists

OUR ALBUM OF BECOMING

As a final reflection, we present the last set of photographs as an album of our becoming.

Gift of Life on Strong Shoulders

Mountain Province, Philippines, 1991
Frans Welman
Courtesy of the Artist

Magdaleno Dueñas: A WWII Veteran Who Helped American Soldiers Escape During the War

San Francisco, California, ca. 1990s
Rick Rocamora
Courtesy of the Artist

Donald Galedo: Letter Carrier for the U.S. Postal Service

Oakland, California, 1990
Lillian Galedo
Courtesy of the Artist

"A Typical Spanish Mestiza"

Philippines, ca. 1913
Anonymous
Dean Worcester, *The Philippines Past and Present*. Vol. 2
(New York: Macmillan Company, 1914).

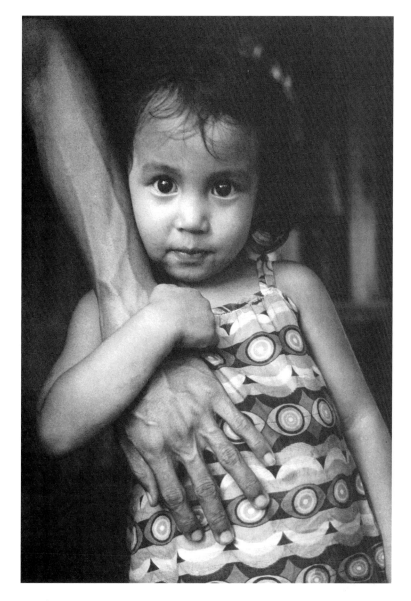

Little Reva

Calbayong, Samar, Eastern Visayas, Philippines, 1979
Lenny Limjoco
Courtesy of the Artist

Pasyon (Passion): "A Member of the Cabaruan Trinity Impersonating Christ and Later Imprisoned for Cattle Stealing"

Cabaruan, Pangasinan, Philippines, ca. 1913
Anonymous
Dean Worcester, *The Philippines Past and Present*. Vol. 2
(New York: Macmillan Company, 1914).

Rebolusyon (Revolution): Bernabe "Commander Dante" Buscayno. As founding member of the rebel New People's Army, he was arrested under the Marcos dictatorship and released when Corazon Aquino came to power in 1986.

Manila, Philippines, 1986
Rick Rocamora
Courtesy of the Artist

Three Muslim Boys with their Prayer Beads Inside a Local Mosque

Zamboanga, Philippines, October 1995
Hiroji Kubota
Editions Didier Millet, Singapore

Three Altar Boys inside Santa Maria Church

Ilocos Sur, Philippines, October 1995
Dominic Sansoni
Editions Didier Millet, Singapore

ABOUT THE CURATORS

Pearlie Rose S. Baluyut
Initially trained as an artist, Baluyut received her B.A. and M.A. in Art History at UCLA, and wrote her thesis on the complexity of Philippine painter Juan Luna's national becoming in Paris during the fin de siècle. She is currently pursuing her Ph.D. in Modern Art, investigating the emergence of art patronage and the reconstruction of national culture in the Philippines under the authoritarian regime of Ferdinand Marcos.

Enrique B. de la Cruz
Describing himself as one of the last Rockefeller Foundation *pensionados*, de la Cruz received his Ph.D. in Philosophy from UCLA. As Assistant Director of the UCLA Asian American Studies Center, he has been involved in various academic endeavors and received a Bayanihan Award for his community service. In conjunction with the 1998 Philippine centennial, he is serving as guest editor for the two-volume commemorative issue of *Amerasia Journal* which focuses on 100 years of Philippine-U.S. relations.

Rico J. Reyes
Reyes earned his B.A. at UC Berkeley and M.F.A. at UCLA where he majored in new and experimental genres. Primarily interested in installation and mixed media, his works pirouette the boundaries of autobiography and conceptual art, exploring issues of memory, identity, and belonging. Besides his participation in art exhibitions in Los Angeles, Manila, New York, and San Francisco, Reyes is actively involved in art education programs.